WILLIAM THE CONQUEROR AND THE NORMANS

Robin May

Illustrations by Gerry Wood

The Bookwright Press
New York · 1985

LIFE AND TIMES

Julius Caesar and the Romans
Alfred the Great and the Saxons
Canute and the Vikings
William the Conqueror and the Normans
Richard the Lionheart and the Crusades
Columbus and the Age of Exploration
Elizabeth I and Tudor England

Further titles are in preparation

First published in the United States in 1985 by
The Bookwright Press
387 Park Avenue South
New York, NY 10016

First published in 1984 by
Wayland (Publishers) Ltd,
49 Lansdowne Place, Hove,
East Sussex BN3 1HF, England

ISBN 0-531-18010-7
Library of Congress Catalog Card Number: 84-73567

Printed by G. Canale & C.S.p.A., Turin, Italy

Contents

1 THE STORY OF WILLIAM THE CONQUEROR

Dangerous years

It was a near miracle that William, Duke of Normandy, lived to win the Battle of Hastings in 1066, that most famous of British dates. William was born in 1028. His father was Robert, Duke of Normandy, his mother a tanner's daughter called Herleva. They were not married, so William was illegitimate. As a result, many powerful nobles believed that William had no right to be Duke of Normandy when his father died — and they were prepared to fight for it. So William's young life was constantly in danger.

Below *When William was a boy his life was often in danger. Here he is seen escaping from some Norman barons who are trying to kill him.*

William's father forced the Norman barons to agree that William should follow him as duke. When Duke Robert died returning from a pilgrimage to Jerusalem in 1035, William became duke in his place. But how could a seven-year-old boy keep tough nobles in order?

The next few years were very hard for young William. One by one, his advisers were murdered. The duchy was torn apart by rebellions and invasions. Fortunately, William had the support of King Henry I of France. Without it, it is doubtful that he would have survived.

William had some narrow escapes. The story is told that the court jester warned William's advisers that the barons were plotting to kill him. No one took any notice of him because he was a clown. So the jester told William himself. William took the threat seriously and escaped to the safety of Falaise Castle. Slowly but surely he gained control of his troublesome duchy. By the age of 20 he was recognized by most Normans as a strong and able leader.

The effigy of Robert, Duke of Normandy, from his tomb in Gloucester Cathedral.

Above In 1066 the Norman invasion fleet set sail for England.

A Norman ship full of soldiers and horses (from the Bayeux Tapestry).

Normandy and England subdued

William's troubles were not yet over. He wanted to marry his cousin Matilda, daughter of the Count of Flanders, but the Pope refused. William had a very strong personality. He took no notice, and as a result was banished from the Catholic Church. All Norman churches were closed down for ten years. Meanwhile, he proved a good husband, a rare thing in those days . . .

In 1054, a vast army of enemies, including his old ally, Henry of France, sought to destroy Normandy and its powerful duke. It was an unwise move. After four years of bitter fighting, William had defeated all his enemies and was the undisputed ruler of Normandy. He and his mounted troops in chain mail became very formidable foes. They also learned the art of building strong castles.

With Normandy subdued, William turned his attention to England. Edward the Confessor was King of England at the time, but it was not clear who should become king after him. William had a strong claim to the throne. His father had been betrothed to Estrith, the sister of King Canute who had ruled England from 1016 to 1035. Also, there is evidence that his claim had been supported by Edward the Confessor and Harold, Earl of Wessex.

Yet on his deathbed in 1066, Edward named the powerful noble Harold as his successor. William was furious. He prepared an invasion force, this time with the Pope's support, for it was believed that Harold had broken his solemn promise. After a closely-fought struggle, William's troops defeated Harold at the Battle of Hastings. So Duke William of Normandy also became King of England by right of conquest.

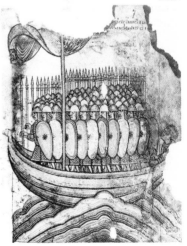

Closely packed Norman soldiers aboard their ship bound for England (from an 11th century manuscript).

7

In 1066 William was crowned King of England at a magnificent ceremony in Westminster Abbey.

Master of England and Normandy

William was crowned King of England in Westminster Abbey on Christmas Day, 1066. A tragedy occurred during the ceremony. The crowds outside the Abbey were making a great noise, shouting and cheering. The Norman guards mistakenly thought that a riot was breaking out so they set fire to the houses round the Abbey, thinking their leader was in danger. It was an omen of the harsh times ahead.

William spent the rest of his life shuttling back and forth between Normandy and England. He had made many enemies and had to be constantly on his guard. By 1071, English resistance to the Normans had been ruthlessly crushed. To make sure that the English were kept quiet, William gave his Norman followers land in key areas of the country. They built castles which overawed

the English. For those English people who lived through the Conquest period, the future seemed wretched.

After 1071, William spent most of his time in Normandy. He was so powerful by now that the French king and the leading French nobles, including his disloyal son Robert, tried to topple him — without success. In 1085, he returned to England to thwart a threatened Viking invasion that never happened.

Two years later, William was back in Normandy to defend it. In 1087, he set fire to a French town called Mantes. In his moment of triumph, William, now enormously fat, was thrown against the pommel of his saddle as his horse reared at burning embers. He fell heavily and died from his injuries.

It is not just as a conqueror that William should be remembered. True, he was a harsh man who fought his way into a position of great power. But he was not simply a brutal soldier. His religious changes proved him to be a good man of the Church while the Domesday Book shows his skill as a leader and an organizer.

A silver penny, dating from 1068, showing the head of William the Conqueror.

9

2 WHO WERE THE NORMANS?

Above *A Norman lady of the manor.*

Normandy was an area in the northeast of France. It had been Viking territory since 911. A few years previously, in 885, Viking longships had sailed up the Seine River, burned Rouen and besieged Paris. From bases by the Seine they extended their influence and power until Charles III, the French king, made a deal with the Viking leader Rollo in 911. As Charles was too weak to expel Rollo, he offered him what became Normandy in return for peace. Normandy is named after the Vikings who are also called "Norsemen."

Rollo became a Christian, and established law and order in the Duchy of Normandy. Although he was supposed to be a subject of the King of France, he was virtually inde-

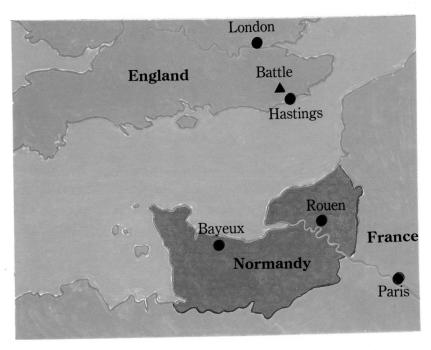

Above *A map showing the position of Normandy in northeast France and in relation to southern England.*

pendent. More Vikings came to live in the duchy. Soon their way of life and speech became French, and they became known as "Normans." Rollo's great-grandson was the most famous Norman of all, William the Conqueror.

The Normans became a brilliant people, combining the strength and daring of their Viking ancestors with the more advanced civilization of the Latin races. They became Christians, builders of magnificent cathedrals, churches and castles, and very fine soldiers and cavalrymen.

Normandy was the most powerful single area in Europe by the Conqueror's time. Like their ancestors, Normans were adventurers long before they set sail for England. Southern Europe would soon find out just how adventurous!

Opposite *The lord of the manor returns to his castle with his family and bodyguard after a morning's sport spent hawking and practicing his archery.*

A fierce-looking Norman baron armed with a battleax, shield and heavy sword.

11

3 NORMANS IN THE MEDITERRANEAN

In southern Italy, Norman adventurers gaze greedily across the Straits of Messina to Sicily, an island they were soon to conquer.

The Normans — like their Viking ancestors — were filled with a spirit of adventure. When Norman pilgrims came back from a visit to Jerusalem in 1015 they brought news that there was action to be had in southern Italy, where families and states were constantly at war.

The younger brothers of Norman families, bored by life at home, set out in search of riches and excitement. Several hundred Norman knights led by Robert Guiscard

(meaning cunning) and his brother, Roger, conquered southern Italy from the Greeks, and Sicily from the Arabs.

The Pope sent an army against these impudent foreigners but it was defeated in 1053. The Normans treated the Pope's messenger for peace so well, that he made an alliance with the formidable newcomers. The Normans must have been remarkable soldiers for so few to have been victorious against so many.

These piratical Normans were not just great fighters: they were also efficient governors. Roger's son, Roger II, ruled both Sicily and Norman territories on the Italian mainland. With the help of English and Greek advisers, he ruled his Kingdom of the Two Sicilies, as it was called. His troops included many Arabs, while Greeks officered his navy. He died in 1154, having presided over a court famous for its arts, learning and sciences.

Above *Two Norman soldiers, similar to the adventurers who went with the Guiscard brothers on their campaigns in southern Italy.*

4 THE CONQUEST OF ENGLAND

Claims to the throne

In 1064, Harold Godwinson was forced by a storm to land in France, where he was captured by a French nobleman. William persuaded the nobleman to surrender his prisoner, and he and Harold, who were distant cousins, became very friendly. It is highly probable that Harold swore over the bones of a holy saint to support William's claim to the English throne.

In a famous scene from the Bayeux Tapestry, Harold Godwinson swears over holy relics to support William's claim to the English throne.

The reigning King of England, Edward the Confessor, had been exiled in Normandy for much of his early life, so he was more of a Norman than an Englishman. He brought many Norman friends to England to the disgust of leading English nobles such as Godwin, Harold's father. Godwin's family were becoming too powerful so that the Normans at Edward's court had Godwin exiled in 1051. In the same year, it is possible that William may have gone to Edward and been promised the Crown of England on Edward's death.

When Godwin and his son Harold returned home from exile, the saintly but weak Edward allowed them to take over the running of the kingdom. Godwin died in 1053, making Harold the most powerful noble in the kingdom. With one of his brothers as Earl of Mercia and another as Earl of Northumbria, it could be said that the Godwin family had England in their pockets.

Edward the Confessor died in 1066. The Witan — the Great Council of England — chose Harold as king, even though he was short on royal blood. Other claimants included King Harald Hardrada of Norway, a great Viking warrior — and Duke William himself.

Opposite *On a visit to Normandy, Harold promises loyalty to Duke William.*

The Battle of Stamford Bridge

THE NORMAN CONQUEST AND MAIN CAMPAIGNS

◯◯◯▶ William's invasion force

▶ Harold's route from Stamford Bridge

▶ 1066-67

▶ 1068

▶ 1070

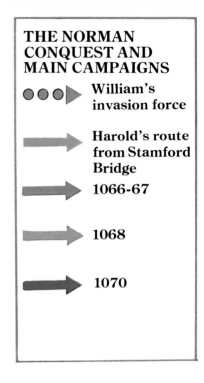

To add to King Harold's problems his brother, Tostig, had turned traitor. Tostig had made himself so unpopular as Earl of Northumbria that he had been driven out. Harold saw no reason to help him, so Tostig decided to join Hardrada. The two men gathered a mighty army and invaded England in the autumn of 1066. They camped at Stamford Bridge, near York.

King Harold hastened north, collecting troops as he went. With him were his housecarls. These were his hand-picked bodyguard, descended from Vikings, but utterly loyal to their king. York had already fallen to the invaders after a hard fight and the men of York agreed to march south with Hardrada to defeat Harold.

On 25 September, Harold found his enemies encamped at Stamford Bridge, ten miles from York. The invaders tried to hold the vital bridge across the River Derwent. Finally, a single Viking was left to stop the English advance until he died a hero's death. The English then crossed the river and a desperate fight began.

The invaders were utterly defeated. Hardrada was killed by an arrow through his throat and Tostig died a death befitting a traitor. It was one of the most crushing blows ever inflicted on the Vikings, from which they never recovered. Hardrada had sailed to England with 300 ships. The survivors could only man twenty. Harold had survived one massive threat, but the real test was to come. Two days after the battle of Stamford Bridge, the Normans sailed for England.

Right *A Viking longship of the type that carried Harald Hardrada's ferocious warriors over the North Sea to England.*

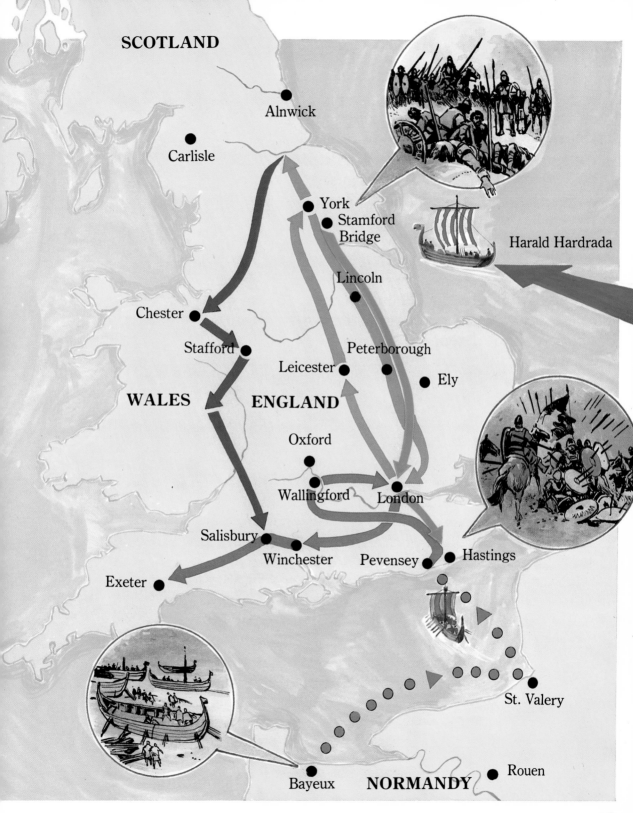

SCOTLAND

Alnwick

Carlisle

York

Stamford
Bridge

Harald Hardrada

Lincoln

Chester

Stafford

Peterborough

Leicester

Ely

WALES

ENGLAND

Oxford

Wallingford

London

Salisbury

Winchester

Pevensey

Hastings

Exeter

St. Valery

Bayeux

NORMANDY

Rouen

The Battle of Hastings

The army that sailed for England on September 27, 1066 was small by today's standards, numbering some 7,000 strong, but it contained some of the finest warriors of the time — Normans from Normandy and Italy, hired troops from Flanders and elsewhere, and some adventurers in search of plunder. The army landed at Pevensey Bay in Sussex on September 8. The future of England hung in the balance.

On October 1, Harold heard the news of the invasion and marched his weary men south. By the 13th, they were face to face with the enemy. Harold might have been wise to have rested his exhausted army and raised more troops, but he was all for action. He, too, had some 7,000 men.

William's army was made up of his feared cavalry, with archers and crossbowmen in support. Harold, though many of his men rode horses, had his army drawn up on foot. There were his loyal housecarls with their great axes, his thanes (knights) and his peasant infantry, the fyrd. The army was defended by its wall of shields.

The battle began early on October 14. The invaders could not break the shield wall, but their furious attacks shook the nerve of some of the fyrd. On one occasion William was unhorsed. His men panicked, until William took off his helmet to show his men he was still alive.

In the end the Normans shot their arrows high into the air. The English soldiers were forced to raise their shields against the hail of arrows raining from the sky. At this moment, the Normans charged again, sweeping away all opposition. Harold and his fiercely loyal housecarls fought until they died. Harold himself was killed, either by an arrow in the eye or hacked to death by Norman swords. At the end of the day, William had won a battle and gained a kingdom.

Opposite *Harold and his loyal housecarls fight to the death at the Battle of Hastings in 1066.*

SENLAC HILL NEAR HASTINGS

Saxon
housecarls

Saxon fyrdmen

London road

Norman archers

Norman infantry

Norman cavalry

The Ravaging of the North

Norman soldiers go on the rampage in northern England, to terrify the Saxons into submission.

William was a great but ruthless man. Arguments still rage as to whether the Conquest was "good" for England or not. In the long run the combination of Saxon, Viking and Norman would make a small island the most powerful nation on earth for many years. But for some, the aftermath of the Conquest was a nightmare.

The new king showed no mercy to his enemies. He expected loyalty and dealt harshly with anyone who resisted him. Terrified by the blood and fire of William's campaign after Hastings, the citizens of London gave in

without a struggle. Within six months William felt confident enough to be able to pay a visit to Normandy.

He was soon back in England to put down a number of rebellions that broke out over a wide area in 1069. The sons of Harold tried to defeat him but William and his local commanders were too good for them. That autumn, however, there was a dangerous uprising in Yorkshire. Prince Edgar, heir to the line of King Alfred, joined the Vikings and captured York.

William hastened north and defeated the rebels. From a base at Nottingham, he launched a campaign of devastation against the north of England. Destruction of human beings, dwellings and crops went on throughout the winter. Tales of the nightmare were told for generations and it took years for the north to recover. As for the Vikings and other contenders for the throne, they had learned their lesson. England was William's — or was it?

Normans set fire to the house of a Saxon family as part of their ruthless campaign to crush a rebellion in the north of England.

Hereward the Wake

Only in the Fens of East Anglia did William meet serious resistance. Nine hundred years ago they were a watery wilderness of islands and swamps, unlike today's tidy farmlands — an ideal place for an English last stand.

Resistance to William was led by a local landowner called Hereward the Wake. He was known as the "watchful one," and the "last of the English" by friend and foe alike. Little is known about Hereward, but he seems to have had a fiery temper, which forced him to leave England before the Conquest. After 1066 he returned to fight William with some Viking allies.

Together, they destroyed Peterborough, but then the Vikings made peace with William. Hereward did not.

The Isle of Ely became the rallying-point for English families who hated the Normans. William was forced to blockade it, and built a causeway across the swamps that became a death road for his men. Finally, Ely's monks, fearing their mainland property would be besieged, betrayed Hereward.

Ely fell to the king, but Hereward escaped, finally making his peace with William who treated him with honor. One story has him dying peacefully, another murdered by jealous Normans after slaying sixteen of them. Whichever is true, the stirring exploits of Hereward the Wake comforted and inspired the conquered English for generations.

Hereward the Wake, the leader of English resistance, escapes from the Isle of Ely where he was surrounded by the Normans.

Above *Three stages in the building of a motte and bailey castle.*

5 THE NORMANS AS BUILDERS

Castles

A Saxon work force builds a mound as part of a Norman motte and bailey castle.

The Normans were famous castle builders. Many of the castles they built are still standing, 800 years later. William needed castles quickly to control his new and rebellious kingdom. He and his barons chose the best sites and destroyed any buildings that stood in their way. For instance, 166 houses were destroyed to make way for Lincoln Castle.

These first castles were rapidly built by the Saxon workforce. Each had a wooden tower on a mound called a motte. It was surrounded by a ditch and stockade. Sometimes the tower was on stilts so that the garrison could move easily below it. Each castle had a big bailey (inner

courtyard). The worst enemy of such a castle was fire. Wooden castles were still built for speed throughout the Norman period, especially during the civil wars of Stephen's reign.

Soon Norman masons were put to work to build castles of stone. A moat was dug if possible, complete with a drawbridge. Walls topped with parapets became higher and thicker, and soon the familiar arrow slits appeared. This gave much greater protection to archers. Later they were cross-shaped, allowing a wider field of fire.

The main building within these magnificent stone castles was the keep, which housed the lord, his family and his men. Several early stone keeps survive to this day in the English countryside. The White Tower of the Tower of London, completed in 1079, is also a classic example of fine Norman architecture.

Norman craftsmen work fast to build a house for their lord.

Castles under siege

Norman soldiers set fire to a fortification they are besieging.

The Normans built castles to defend themselves against foreign invasions and rebellions within England itself. They proved very effective. There was no way in which the local English could challenge the Normans in their castles unless they were prepared to risk execution or torture in a dark, rat-infested dungeon.

It was not easy for besiegers to capture a castle in this period. Yet it was possible, as King Stephen proved in 1138 when he laid seige to Shrewsbury Castle. He eventually took it by setting fire to brushwood in the ditch in front of the castle. The garrison was smoked out and more than ninety of them were hanged.

The best chance of success was the presence of a

traitor within the walls, starving a garrison into submission, or undermining the walls. Battering rams, scaling ladders, siege towers, and machines that hurled everything from stones to rotting carcasses were used, but not always with success. In Norman times, such siege equipment was still quite primitive.

Castles proliferated in England's first civil war. It seems that by the year 1150, there were more than 1,100 castles in England. Many of them were built illegally, without the permission of the king. Cathedrals were sometimes turned into castles. Hereford Cathedral was besieged in 1140. Stones and arrows rained down from the cathedral tower upon the heads of the attackers in the cemetery. Matilda turned the church tower of Bampton in Oxfordshire into a castle. Her enemy Stephen did the same to St. Mary's in Chester.

During the Norman period, many formidable stone castles were built. To increase the chances of success when besieging a castle, the attackers started to use terrifying weapons — like this stone-throwing catapult — to batter down the walls.

Cathedrals

In the years following the Conquest, the Normans started a huge building program. Apart from their castles, church building was carried out on a vast scale. Cathedrals and abbeys crowned their work.

William the Conqueror founded Battle Abbey in Sussex in honor of his nearby victory over Harold. Other abbeys and cathedrals were built under the supervision of abbots and bishops. Some bishops, like St. Hugh of Lincoln, even helped his workers by carrying stones. A huge workforce was needed. Masons cut and shaped great blocks of stone, carpenters carved wood, glaziers worked

An architect discusses the building of St. John's Chapel in the Tower of London.

A beautifully carved capital from Hyde Abbey, Winchester dating back to 1130.

with glass for the windows, and artists painted the walls and decorated the tombs with jewelry. Today's detailed architectural plans did not exist — few craftsmen could read anyway. What counted was skill and a sharp eye, especially to create the rounded arch which is such a common feature of Norman churches and cathedrals.

Sometimes enthusiasm got the better of skill. Norman towers occasionally fell down. Bishop Walkelin of Winchester had to endure that shame. William Rufus, the son of William I, was unfairly blamed for the disaster by some because it was known that he was not religious. This view is hardly fair because it was he who started Westminster Hall, some of his work remaining to this day.

Many would claim that Durham Cathedral, built from 1093 to 1133, is the finest example of Norman architecture in England. Along with the Norman castle nearby and the glorious setting, it forms one of the supreme examples of Norman building skills anywhere in Europe. Apart from Durham, there are many other magnificent cathedrals and impressive castles still standing. To this day, they remain an important symbol of the skill and power of the Normans.

The mason who helped monks to build All Saints Church, Buncton, West Sussex in 1150, carved his own figure into the stonework. The church is mentioned in the Domesday Book as Botechitoune.

6 THE NORMANS IN CONTROL

Feudalism at work

Above *A farm worker.*

Villeins worked hard to harvest crops for the lord of the manor.

In the Dark Ages after the fall of the Roman Empire around the year 500, law and order crumbled in Europe. Barbarian tribes roamed the countryside, stealing what they pleased and behaving as they wished. Fearing for their lives, people flocked to strong leaders for protection. It was natural that those leaders would want more than thanks. What they wanted was loyalty and service in war.

The feudal system grew out of this lawless situation. It was designed to benefit both the leaders and the people they led. Society was divided into layers. At the top was the king. He owned all the land in the country but he leased most of it out to his great lords. These tenants-in-chief promised to be loyal to the king and fight for him in gratitude for his protection, justice and the use of land.

These great lords kept some land for themselves and leased the rest out to sub-tenants — lesser lords, knights and sheriffs — expecting loyalty and support in return.

On the bottom layer were villeins. In return for protection, they worked as hard as slaves on their lord's land. Occasionally they were able to call a small strip of land their own. Land that was held from a feudal lord was called a "fief": the word "feudal" comes from the Latin for fief.

By the 14th century the system was dying. A new breed of professional longbowmen, for instance, were not feudal servants. The Black Death of that century almost finished the system off. Those peasants who survived the Black Death demanded wages, to be paid in cash or kind for the work they did. Feudalism was finished by 1500. It was no longer needed, but it had served a useful purpose during those lawless years of the Dark Ages.

Below *As part of the feudal system, a peasant had to give some of his crops to the lord in return for protection of his life, land and family.*

The Domesday Book

It was at Christmas in 1085 that William the Conqueror decided to have his famous Domesday Book compiled. The result was the most complete survey of property — of the wealth of the nation — that was compiled anywhere in Europe during the whole of the Middle Ages. It told the king who owned what, how much the king could get from his land tax, and how many troops he could raise.

The name "Domesday" was added after William's death. It refers to the Day of Judgement, which some people believe we must face when we die. Just as death is unavoidable, so too was any attempt to try and dodge tax once the Domesday Book had been completed!

A piece of writing from the Domesday Book about Westminster Abbey.

The king sent out royal commissioners to visit every shire (or county) in the land. They used shire courts as their headquarters. From there, they issued a series of questions about who held the land and who worked it. They also asked how much it was worth before 1066; how much at the time when the new land-holder received it from William; and, finally, its current value. Lists were made of the king's property, and of land held by the Church and the leading tenants-in-chief. It also listed those women who held property, land still held by English thanes, and so on down the scale. The information filled two big volumes. Details included the numbers of ox teams and villeins at work on each property.

Not everyone was pleased about such a survey being made. There were some riots over the invasion of privacy and the high rate of taxation. But from William's point of view, it was very useful, resulting in a highly efficient taxation system — and it supplied a wealth of knowledge about the Norman period for us today.

Churches and monks

Lanfranc, Archbishop of Canterbury from 1070 to 1089, visits a monastery.

Religion played a great part in the life of the people of England — and most of Europe — in Norman times. Vast numbers of men and women left the outside world to become monks and nuns. Outside the walls of monasteries and nunneries, religion was flourishing too and had a powerful influence on the lives of the people.

There was a great surge of religious feeling in Norman times. The Pope had blessed William's invasion so the English Church looked favorably upon the king. He made his Norman friend, Lanfranc, Archbishop of Canterbury. Lanfranc tightened up standards in monasteries and encouraged Norman priests and monks to cross the Channel to live and work in England.

Monasteries were houses of prayer, but they served many other purposes. They were used as resting-places for weary travelers, and as hospitals for the sick. They also became centers for education and learning.

A monk's day was long and tiring and the discipline was strict. They were usually out of bed by 2 a.m. for the first service of the day. They then worked and prayed all day until they retired to bed at 7 p.m. It is not surprising that many youngsters who joined a monastery became fed up with the harsh and disciplined life. Sometimes they delighted in causing scandals. Yet many liked the life and made the best of their free education.

Outside monasteries, most judges and government officials were also part-time priests known as "secular" clergy. The Church as an organization had great power and independence which was to cause many problems for later kings of England.

Below *This wall painting from St. Peter and St. Paul Church, in Chaldon, Surrey, dates from 1200. The bottom layer shows hell; the top layer, Heaven. People can be seen scrambling up a ladder to escape the fires of hell.*

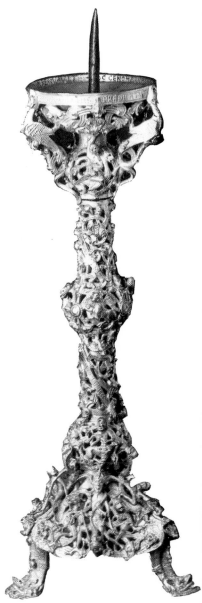

Above *The Gloucester candlestick, beautifully worked in gold.*

Law and order

Sometimes, men involved in a dispute had to fight to the death in a "trial by battle."

The Norman Conquest split England in two — foreign rulers and native ruled. Norman rulers lorded it over a defeated people, despising the native English language. Yet fortunately for the English, the early Norman kings had the good sense to look to the Anglo-Saxons in times of crisis to help them keep powerful Norman barons in order. When William II ran into trouble, it was his "brave and honorable English" who helped him take the revels. Anglo-Saxons knew the danger to themselves of a weak king.

Before the Conquest, much Saxon law had been concerned with stopping blood feuds between families. A system of fines had been introduced to prevent families wiping each other out. Another important part of Saxon law were the "ordeals." The accused had to plunge his arm into boiling water. If after three days his bandaged arm had healed properly, he was innocent!

The Normans, fearful of being murdered by those they oppressed, made rebellious communities pay heavy fines. As hatred of the Normans increased, the Normans used more vicious punishments. Hangings and mutilations became commonplace. The Normans also introduced a trial by combat. The two people involved in an argument had to fight to the death. It was assumed that whoever survived was innocent. This grossly unfair system led many to volunteer to pay fines while others took refuge in churches, where they could not be harmed.

What really mattered in these dangerous times was that the king should be strong and able. That tough Norman king, Henry I, had to work hard to earn his title of "Lion of Justice."

Opposite *These men are running for their lives because they know that there are brutal punishments for anyone caught poaching deer in the King's forest.*

7 DAILY LIFE

Town life

London was the most important town in Norman times. It had a population of perhaps 10,000, making it twice as big as any other Norman town. It was a lively place, with a bustling fish market, a weekly horse fair, and many fine stores. Unluckily for us, it was not mentioned in the Domesday Book, but there are many later descriptions of it. One such description tells of a special official in charge of refuse disposal, a nasty but vital job in medieval times. The royal treasure was in London, and the town was still an important religious and educational center.

Some towns were started by a lord, once he had got royal permission to hold a market. England had been a great trading nation before the Conquest and this continued. English cloth, for instance, was popular in Europe. The ravaging of the North, however, set towns like York and Chester back for some years. No

Below Norman shoppers in the market ask a blacksmith to hammer out a metal utensil for use in their homes.

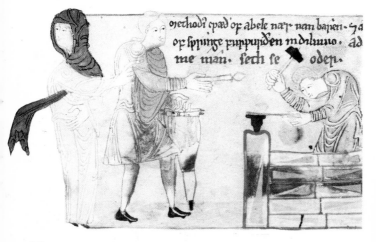

towns were big by modern standards. Lincoln, for instance, had only 730 houses in 1086. Norwich did not have many more houses and yet by 1086 it had 20 churches and 43 chapels.

The Conqueror believed that trouble easily brewed in towns which is why he built castles to dominate them. However, towns produced wealth and many were granted charters once things had settled down, giving them privileges. It was a way of ensuring bigger populations and profits. By the 12th century many towns were booming.

Below *Most Norman towns had markets like this one where it was possible to buy food, clothes and many other goods.*

Country life

In Norman times there were two centers of village life, the manor house, and the church. Most country folk were villeins. They led a hard and thankless life, working long hours and eating sparingly. After a breakfast of bread and ale, work on the lord's farm began.

A reeve was in charge of the village's work, while a steward ran things if the lord of the manor was away. Villeins plowed with ox-teams, oxen being strong and cheap to feed. The lord's work had to be done before those villagers with a little land could do their own. The villagers could also use common land for grazing their livestock. Only in autumn was there fresh meat, when animals not needed for breeding or plowing were killed.

Pigs were ideal animals to keep as they could feed themselves.

The poorest villagers lived in one-room hovels and slept on rushes or straw on the floor. A little prosperity brought a longer house and a loft; a little more allowed for banishment of the bigger animals to a special building; dogs, chickens and pigs were allowed to remain in the house. So you can imagine that houses in Norman times were far from clean!

The Church — without seating — was a lively spot for village meetings as well as services, and the churchyard was a place to buy and sell. Despite the Domesday Book, though, we can only get a hazy picture of life in a Norman village where most villagers spent their entire lives.

Below *A villein works on the corn harvest.*

Battlements

Dormitories

Great hall

Chapel

Well

Store room

Spiral staircase to dungeon

Life in a Norman castle

Above *A scene from a lively feast held in a nobleman's great hall.*

Looking at the remains of early castles, we find them dark and dismal places to live. Yet castle dwellers were far better off than most people. Some castles were palaces as well and most were fortress homes.

The castle was the home of the lord, his lady and family, and the castle servants. The lord and his family had their own suite of rooms. Castle servants would sleep around the fire at night in the great hall, either on rushes on the floor or on benches.

Meals in the great hall were bustling and noisy occasions. Trestle tables were put up for the guests, with the lord sitting at the high table with his closest friends. Servants brought in steaming dishes which the guests ate with their fingers until they could eat no more. The atmosphere must have been smoky without chimneys, smoke exiting through holes in the walls or window openings. There were no glass windows, but shutters could be put up to keep out the drafts.

Living conditions in a castle were crude. Sanitation was basic. Toilets were simply a shaft in the wall, if possible over a moat or stream. A cask or barrel of water was used for the occasional bath, but mostly the Normans went unwashed.

To a modern person, Norman castles would have seemed cold and uncomfortable and there was a high risk of disease. Yet with its kitchen, sleeping quarters, chapel, well, workshop and, often, its decorated walls, the Norman castle was an oasis of comfort in a hard era.

Opposite *A cut-away drawing of the inside of a Norman castle showing the most important places within it.*

Above *The lord of the manor rides from his castle for an afternoon's hawking.*

Sports and entertainment

The Norman Conquest, grim as it was, could not stop people enjoying themselves when they got the chance. The favorite sport of Normans was mock warfare. Young Normans, hoping for knighthood, not only fought among themselves but were prepared to challenge Londoners to fights with lances and shields.

There were less brutal forms of entertainment too. The music of minstrels, morris dancing and dancing around the maypole were popular. Miracle or mystery plays could be seen in churches and market places. Indoor games included chess and dice. Music, in churches and outside, was much enjoyed.

An early form of soccer was played with unlimited numbers of players, sometimes village versus village, while in winter animal bones formed good skates. Schoolboys went in for cockfighting, their elders for bull and boar baiting. Before the Conquest, people could hunt anywhere. William I "loved the tall stags like a father," and turned vast areas of countryside into royal forests. Anyone caught poaching a deer there would be blinded. Just to be caught in a forest with arrows or dogs meant savage punishment.

Above *A group of musicians playing some instruments popular at that time.*

Right *A knight goes into action, lance ready to strike.*

In a sporting contest, two knights on horseback battle it out with lances and shields.

8 LATER NORMAN KINGS

William Rufus

William Rufus lies dead in the New Forest with an arrow in his heart. No one is sure who fired the fatal shaft.

William Rufus got his name from his red face. When his father, William I, died in 1087, William Rufus took charge in England. His incompetent brother, Robert, received Normandy, his other brother Henry, nothing but riches.

William was faced with a difficult situation. Many barons had lands in England and Normandy, which split their loyalties. A rebellion in England failed because William

promised free hunting, less taxation and better government, promises he soon forgot when the crisis was over.

William tried to steal Normandy from Robert. He need not have troubled because his brother sold the duchy to William to raise money for a crusade. However, when Robert returned with a rich bride, he wanted Normandy back.

Before a crisis occurred, William was killed in the New Forest by an arrow. His other brother, Henry, was with him and raced to Winchester to secure the royal treasury. Within three days, he was crowned. William's death is a great mystery. One of the hunting party, Walter Tyrel, fled abroad, having perhaps shot the arrow. Was Henry involved in the murder? Perhaps we shall never know but whatever the truth, a better man now reigned.

William Rufus, taken from a 14th century manuscript.

Henry I: the Lion of Justice

Whatever his involvement in the death of his brother, Henry I gave the English good government and was a great believer in keeping law and order. It was said of him that "no man durst misdo against another in his time," high praise in those dangerous days. His wife Matilda was descended from Alfred the Great, which delighted the English. Intermarriage between Normans and English became quite common from this time.

Henry had a gift for government. He created England's first Civil Service to run the nation under his guidance and keep the great quarrelsome nobles in order. These "civil servants" were chosen from among the less important nobles. They stayed at Westminster while Henry traveled all over his kingdom settling disputes.

Henry had trouble with his brother Robert, Duke of Normandy, who claimed his throne. But Robert was no match for Henry, who paid him to leave England. As Robert was still not satisfied, Henry invaded Normandy and defeated his brother at the Battle of Tinchebrai in 1106. Henry put him in a comfortable prison and became master of Normandy as well as England.

Unlike William Rufus, Henry tried to get along with the Church. He reinstated Anselm, who had been unable to get along with William, as Archbishop of Canterbury. However, Henry fell out with him over who should have control over the Church. Henry wanted bishops to swear loyalty to him and receive their rings and staffs of office from him. Anselm objected, but Henry won, after a long struggle.

A zodiac sign showing the Libran scales of justice, taken from the Hunterian Psalter, dating from 1170.

Below *In an open-air court Henry I listens to the arguments of two men in a dispute before deciding which of them deserves to win the case.*

Above *Henry I from his Great Seal.*

Above *Henry I laments the death of his son in the wreck of the "White Ship." (from a 12th century family tree).*

The "White Ship"

Henry I, who believed so strongly in good government, knew how important it was to have an heir to the English throne. He had one legitimate son, Prince William. In 1120, the king returned from a visit to Normandy ahead of his son, who followed shortly afterwards in the "White Ship." Also aboard were William's half-brother and half-sister, many lords and ladies, and the royal treasure. Tragically, the ship struck a rock and sank off the Normandy coast. All aboard were drowned except a butcher from Rouen in Normandy.

When the news reached England, Henry's courtiers, many of whom had lost loved ones, could not bring themselves to tell the king for a whole day. Then the young son of a count knelt before the king and broke the news. Henry fell senseless and it is said that he never smiled again.

This was a double tragedy for the hard-working monarch. He had lost his son and knew that when he died there would be a struggle for the crown which would destroy the law and order he had worked so hard to achieve. Such a struggle could undo his life's work. True, he was a despot, but that was no bad thing in Norman times as long as a ruler was just.

When Henry died in 1135 from a fever after eating too many fish called lampreys, thirty years of peace came to an end. Now there were two contenders for the Crown of England — and one of them was a woman.

Opposite *As the "White Ship" runs aground, its terrified occupants dive overboard into a smaller boat. Sad to say, this boat capsized too, and Henry I's beloved son and heir, William the Atheling, was drowned.*

The Civil War

Who would succeed Henry now that his son was dead? There were two candidates, Henry's daughter Matilda — and Stephen, whose mother was the Conqueror's daughter. Matilda was tough and able but the Normans were unhappy about accepting a woman ruler. However, Henry's nobles swore to be true to her.

Soon after Henry's death, however, England was plunged into a civil war so awful that a monk wrote that it was said, "Christ and his saints were asleep." Stephen had reached London first. Aided by his brother, the Bishop of Winchester, he was crowned king. His enemies included many of the nobility, churchmen and Henry's civil servants. But he had the crown in his grasp.

Matilda, already in control of Normandy, came to England. What Henry had feared now happened. The barons took control of their own areas. English unity was fractured. Anarchy reigned and famine and plague swept the land.

Stephen was captured in 1141. Matilda became queen but she upset Londoners by taxing them too heavily. They supported Stephen's wife when she marched on the capital. Stephen was freed in exchange for three leading nobles and he attacked Oxford, forcing Matilda to flee from its castle in the snow. There was a lull after Matilda retreated to Normandy in 1148. Seeking to regain the throne, her twenty-year-old son Henry invaded England and was doing well when Stephen's heir died. For once, common sense prevailed. Nobles and clergy decided that Stephen should reign until his death, then Henry should have the throne. Stephen, the last of the Norman kings, died in 1154. England gained one of her greatest kings, Henry Plantagenet, who became Henry II.

Above *and* **below** *The two sides of a coin, minted during King Stephen's reign from 1135 to 1154.*

Opposite *Under cover of a snow blizzard, Matilda escapes from Oxford Castle during the civil war between herself and King Stephen.*

52

9 NORMAN ACHIEVEMENTS

How great do the Normans' achievements seem to us today? A century ago they seemed very great. But recently, much has been learned about the civilization of our Anglo-Saxon ancestors. When put side-by-side with the Saxons, the achievements of the Normans who conquered them do not seem so significant.

Yet the Normans, invading at a time when England had been gravely weakened by poor government, gave much to the land they conquered. They brought strong government, Stephen's dismal reign apart. They were most efficient governors and the Domesday Book is a remarkable testimony to their skill for organization. Feudalism, though hardly a friendly institution, worked well. They were great builders who left behind them magnificent castles and cathedrals as visible proof of their building prowess.

The link with Normandy was strong, with officials regularly crossing the channel keeping England a part of Europe. At Bayeux in Normandy a supreme achievement of the Normans can be found. It is the Bayeux Tapestry, which so vividly shows the events leading up to the Conquest and the Conquest itself.

The Normans improved the religious life of the nation. They were great warriors who proved the importance of cavalry. Normans, invaders themselves, ended the threat of Viking invasions. They were ruthless men in a ruthless age, none more so than the most powerful and successful Norman of them all, William the Conqueror.

William the Conqueror's Great Seal.

Opposite *The leading figures of the Norman Age — William the Conqueror and Henry I — and the major achievements of the Normans: the castle, monastic life, the mounted knight, the Bayeux Tapestry and the Domesday Book.*

HARO LD REX : INTERFEC TVS:EST

Table of dates

885 Vikings besiege Paris in France.

911 The Viking, Rollo, becomes the first Duke of Normandy.

1028 William the Conqueror, Rollo's great-grandson, is born.

1051 Edward the Confessor, King of England from 1042-1066, promises English throne to William?

1053 Normans in Italy defeat the army of Pope Leo IX.

1066 Edward the Confessor dies.
Harold Godwinson is elected king.
Battle of Stamford Bridge. The Viking, Harald Hardrada, and Harold's brother, Tostig, are defeated and killed by King Harold's troops.
Battle of Hastings. William the Conqueror defeats King Harold. Harold is killed in battle and William the Conqueror becomes king.

1069-70 William crushes rebellions in the north of England.

1070-71 Hereward the Wake resists the Normans on the Isle of Ely.

1085 William orders the compilation of the Domesday Book.

1087 William the Conqueror dies.
William Rufus becomes King of England.

1092 Bayeux Tapestry completed.

1100 William II is killed in a hunting "accident" in the New Forest.
Henry I (William II's brother) becomes king.

1106 Battle of Tinchebrai. Henry defeats his brother, Robert, and becomes the undisputed Duke of Normandy.

1120 The wreck of the "White Ship." Henry's only son, and the heir to the throne, is drowned.

1127 Henry's daughter, Matilda, is recognized as heir to the throne by the leading barons.

1128 Matilda marries Geoffrey Plantagenet.

1133 Building of Durham Cathedral is completed.

1135 Henry I dies.
Stephen, Henry I's nephew, seizes the throne.

1139 Matilda lands in England to claim the throne.

1141 Civil war breaks out between Stephen and Matilda.

1148 Matilda leaves England and returns to Normandy where her husband, Geoffrey, is now duke.

1151 Henry Plantagenet, son of Matilda and Geoffrey, succeeds his father as Count of Anjou and Duke of Normandy.

1154 On the death of Stephen, Henry Plantagenet becomes Henry II, King of England.

New words

Bailey The courtyard of a castle surrounded by a high wall.

Blood feuds Fierce arguments and disagreements between families, leading to bloodshed.

Cavalry Soldiers who fought on horseback.

Chain mail A piece of armor worn by knights, made from interlocking pieces of metal.

Civil servants People employed to help with the day-to-day running of government.

Civil war War fought between people of the same nationality.

Court The place where the king stayed, or the people (courtiers) who spent their lives in attendance on the king.

Court jester A clown or joker who kept the king amused at court.

Drawbridge A castle door that could be lowered over a moat to form a bridge.

Duchy Territory governed by a duke.

Dungeon A cellar beneath a castle, used to imprison people.

Exiled Banished from one's own country and not allowed to return.

Feudal System A system of government which split society into groups. Each group had its duties and responsibilities to the other groups.

Fief A piece of land given to a tenant in return for loyalty and service in war.

Fyrd Saxon peasant soldiers.

Glazier A craftsman who made glass for cathedral windows.

Housecarl King Harold's hand-picked bodyguard of Saxon soldiers.

Hovel A very poor dwelling place.

Keep The strongest and best-defended part of a castle.

Latin races People descended from the Romans, who live close to the Mediterranean or in South America.

Mason A craftsworker who carves stone.

Maypole A tall pole, used in Mayday celebrations, around which people danced holding streamers joined to its top.

Minstrel A traveling musician and singer.

Moat A water-filled ditch surrounding a castle.

Morris dancing An ancient form of English folk dancing.

Motte A mound of earth forming the strongest part of early Norman castles.

Oath A binding promise.

Pilgrim A person who makes a special journey to a holy place.

Pope The spiritual leader of the Catholic Church, based in Rome.

Reeve A man put in charge of seeing that the villeins worked hard on their lord's property.

Shire court A place in each county where law cases were tried.

Tapestry A heavy cloth with pictures woven into it, often telling a story, as in the Bayeux Tapestry.

Tenants-in-Chief The most important men in the country who had their land from the king himself.

Thane A Saxon nobleman.

Villein A peasant who worked for the lord of the manor as an agricultural laborer.

Further information

Cameron, A. *Living Under the Normans.*
New York: Longman, 1978.

Crossley-Holland, Kevin C. *Green Blades
Rising: The Anglo-Saxons.* Boston:
Houghton Mifflin, 1976.

Davison, Brian. *Explore A Castle.* North
Pomfret, VT: David & Charles, 1983.

Denny, Norman and Filmer-Sankey,
Josephine. *Bayeux Tapestry: The Norman
Conquest 1066.* Topsfield, MA: Merrimack
Publications Circle, 1984.

Gallagher, Maureen. *The Cathedral Book.*
Ramsey, NJ: Paulist Press, 1983.

Macauley, David. *Cathedral: The Story of Its
Construction.* Boston: Houghton Mifflin,
1973.

Peach, L. Dugarde. *William the Conqueror.*
Bedford Hills, NY: Merry Thoughts,
1968.

Place, Robin. *The Vikings.* New York:
Warwick Press/Franklin Watts, 1980.

Rooke, Patrick, et al. *The Normans.* Morris-
town, NJ: Silver Burdett, 1978.

Index

Picture acknowledgments

The illustrations in this book are supplied by: BBC Hulton Picture Library 52; Glasgow University Library 13, 44 (top), 49 (top); Mansell Collection 5, 11, 15, 21, 24; John Topham Picture Library 54; S. Peter and S. Paul Church, Chaldon, Surrey; Stephen White-Thomson 29 (bottom); Victoria and Albert Museum 35. The remaining photographs are from the Wayland Picture Library.